THE DEEP END

For my grandparents

AUTHOR'S NOTE:

The ocean is scary. It's dark, deep, and full of things that can eat you. Humans are not designed for the deep ocean; we're much more comfortable atop the waves than below them. That makes the work of the intrepid explorers who took it upon themselves to venture into the briny deep all the more impressive. Humans have been wandering the ocean for thousands of years. From early Polynesian explorers who set off over thousands of miles of open ocean in dugout canoes to modern-day adventurers inventing technology that allows us to examine what remains a vast, unexplored undersea wilderness, I stand in awe of the courage and determination it takes to dive into the great unknown. I hope after seeing some of their discoveries in the pages ahead, you will too.

PS: If you could read all of Brownbeard's lines in your best pirate voice, that would be great.

DREW SHENEMAN

THE DEEP END

REAL FACTS ABOUT THE OCEAN

HARPER

An Imprint of HarperCollinsPublishers

Even though water covers almost three-quarters of our planet, the world beneath the waves remains mostly unexplored.

We know you've traveled the globe, sailing the seas, but have you ever wondered what lies beneath the waves?

NOT PERSONALLY, NO.

HE'S NOT A STRONG SWIMMER. AWK!

There are wonders below the surface more amazing than any treasure.

Don't believe me? Ask a scientist!

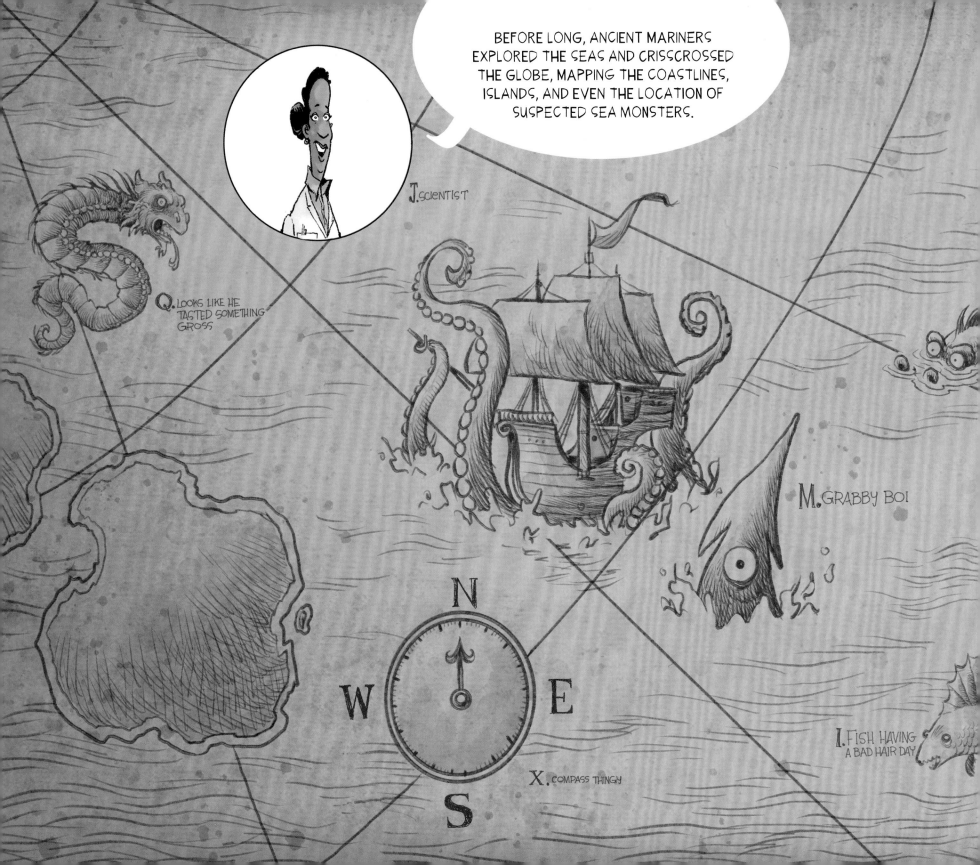

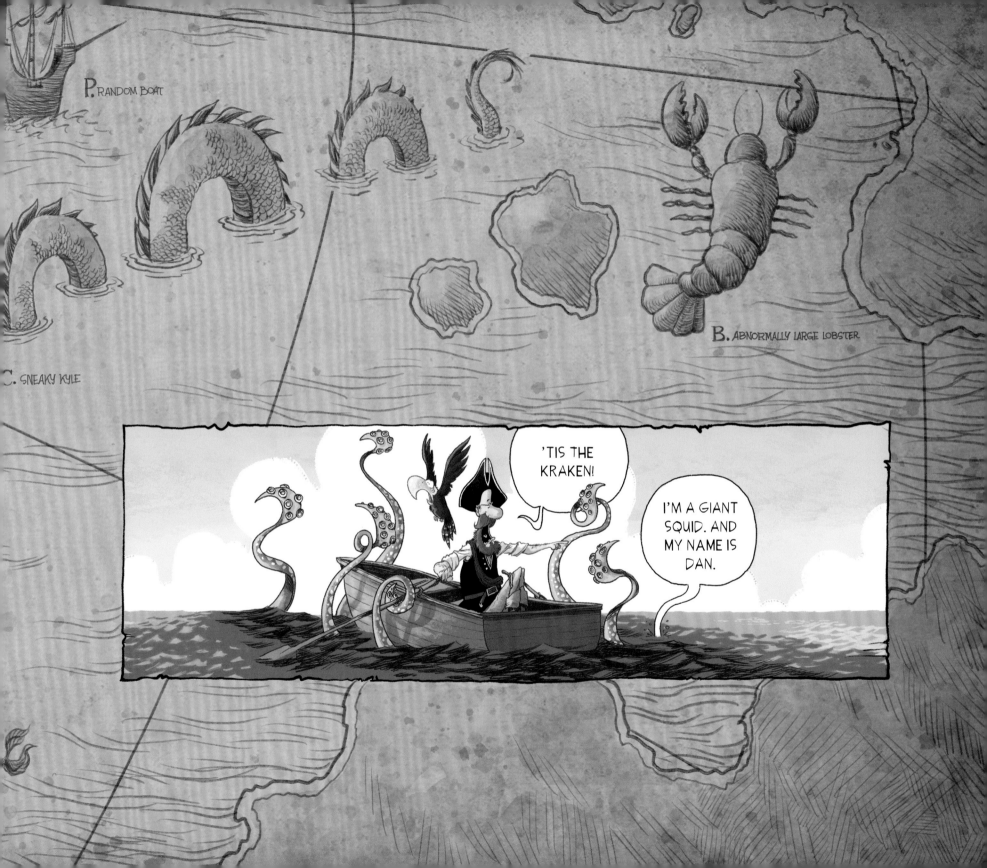

Explorers wanted to venture into the deep,
but first they had to figure out how.

Have you ever held a cup upside down
underwater to trap the air? Now imagine you're
inside the cup. That's basically a diving bell.

Diving bells have been used for thousands of years.
They allowed humans to travel underwater and stay
there. For a little while, at least.

As you can imagine, being lowered into the sea in an upside-down bucket until your ears pop was very dangerous, so most exploration continued to be done while on board a ship.

AFTER YOU.
I REALLY,
REALLY INSIST.

FUN FACT:

Oceanography is the study of the ocean, and modern oceanography started in 1872 with the voyage of the HMS *Challenger*, a British expedition to measure just about everything they could about the ocean, including temperature, current, and depth.

THEY EVEN DISCOVERED THE DEEPEST KNOWN SPOT IN THE ENTIRE OCEAN AND NAMED IT THE CHALLENGER DEEP.

THE CHALLENGER DEEP IS ALMOST 36,000 FEET BELOW THE SURFACE. THAT'S NEARLY SEVEN MILES!

CHALLENGER

The anglerfish uses bioluminescence—glowing in the dark—to attract food.

Tube worms use a process called chemosynthesis to consume the minerals on deep-sea thermal vents. Minerals are the stuff that make up rocks.

The yeti crab uses the fine setae, or hairs, on its arms to filter and feed on tiny bacteria.

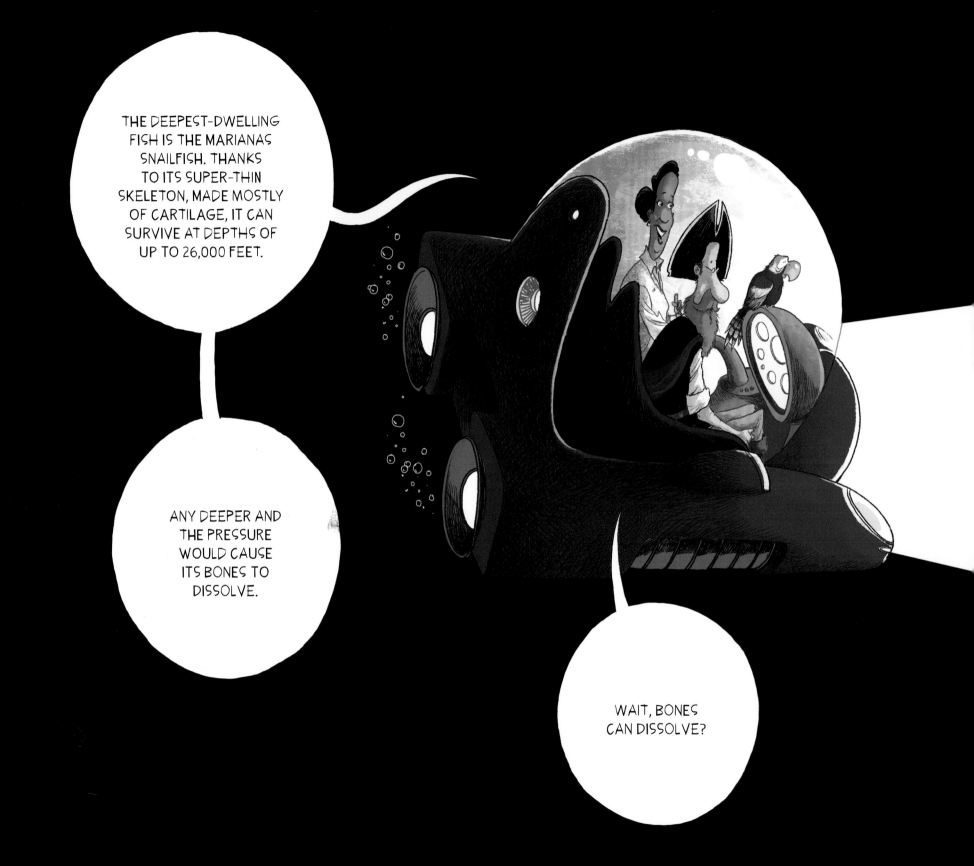

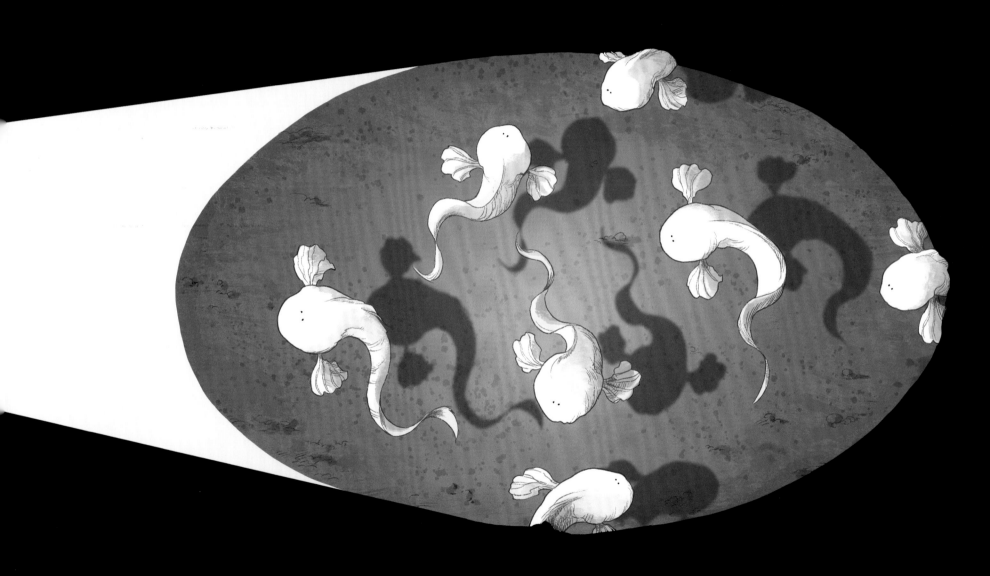

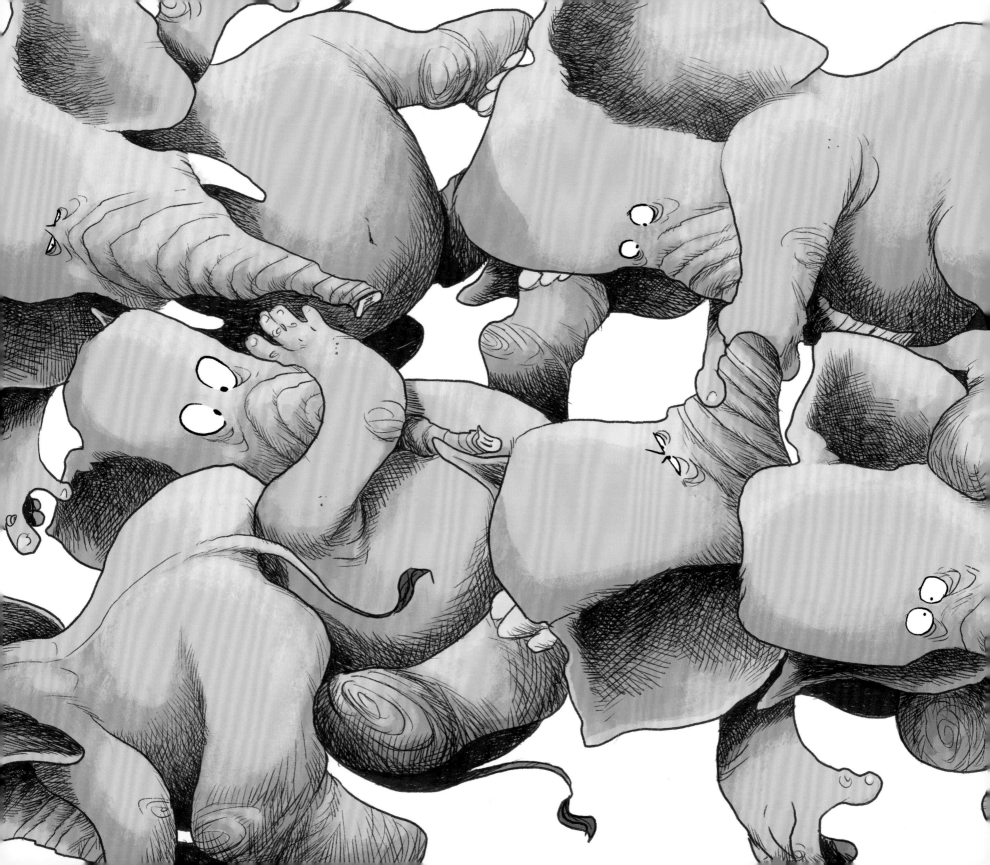

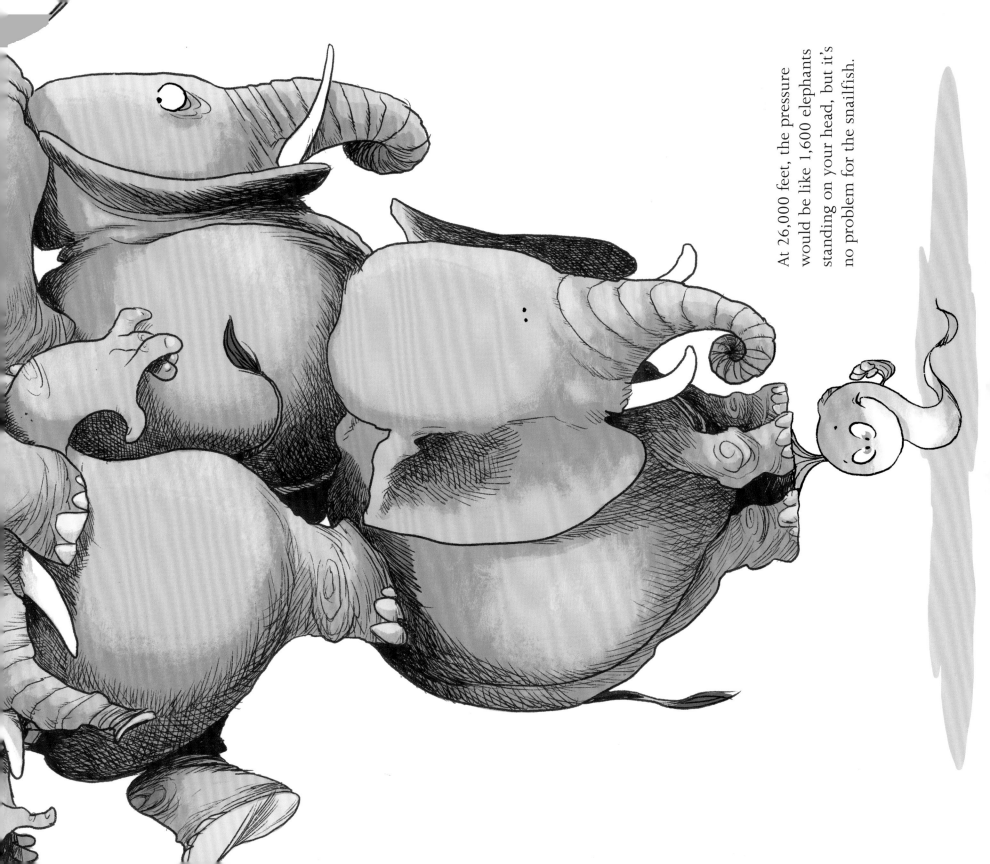

At 26,000 feet, the pressure would be like 1,600 elephants standing on your head, but it's no problem for the snailfish.

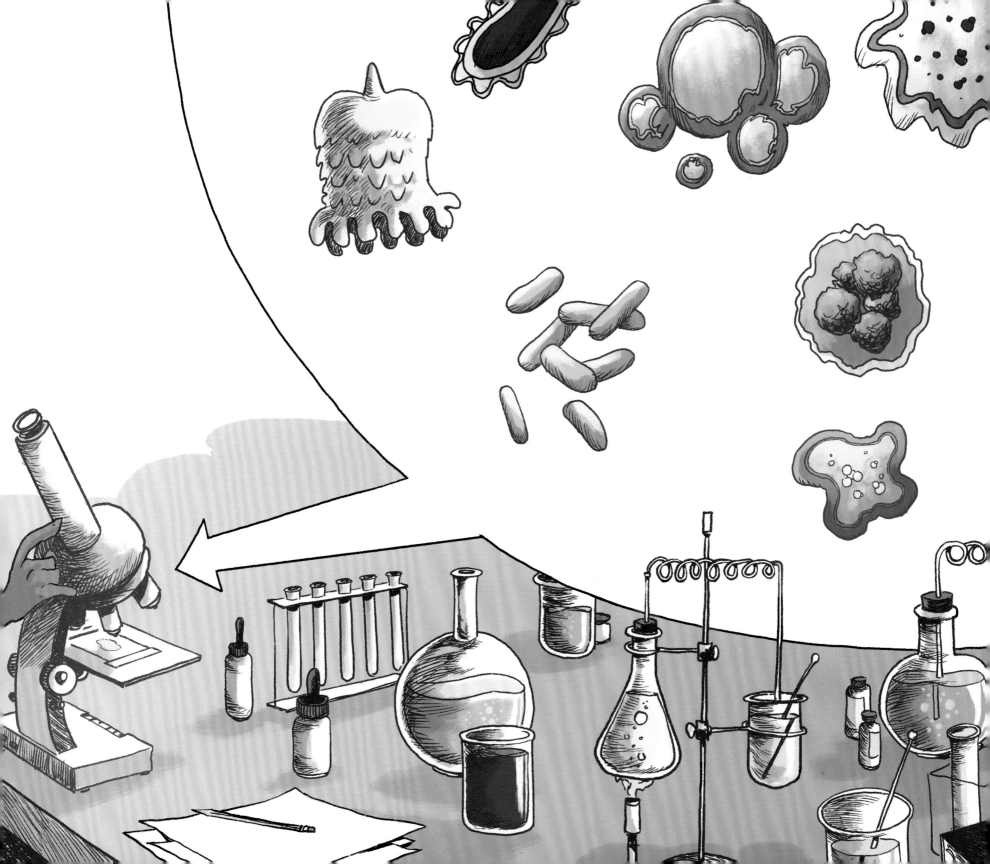

Exploring a frigid, pitch-black environment can pose some interesting challenges for scientists.

SO YOU'RE TELLING ME MY SNORKEL ISN'T GOING TO CUT IT?

One way we explore the ocean depths is with sonar, a method for using sound waves to locate objects in the water.

It's a technique used by dolphins, bats, and Leonardo da Vinci!

In 1490, da Vinci figured out he could put a tube in the water that allowed him to hear far-off ships.

Sound can go places light can't. Scientists bounce sound waves off the ocean floor and measure the time it takes to travel back.

This allows us to paint a pretty accurate image of the seafloor.

I USE SONAR TO FIND BUGS.

But that's not the only method we have to explore the deep.

The first submarine was built in 1620. It was made of wood, iron, and leather and could dive to a depth of 15 feet.

Today we have submersibles that can dive to the very bottom of the sea. Some have pilots and some are remote controlled.

SO THEY DON'T NEED TO BORROW THE SNORKEL?

AWK! YOU'RE BEING REALLY WEIRD ABOUT THE SNORKEL.

THE ALVIN DEEP-SEA SUBMERSIBLE IS ABLE TO DIVE TO 21,000 FEET.

Scientists can go deeper and stay longer than they could in the past.

That's crucial because ocean exploration is now more important than ever.

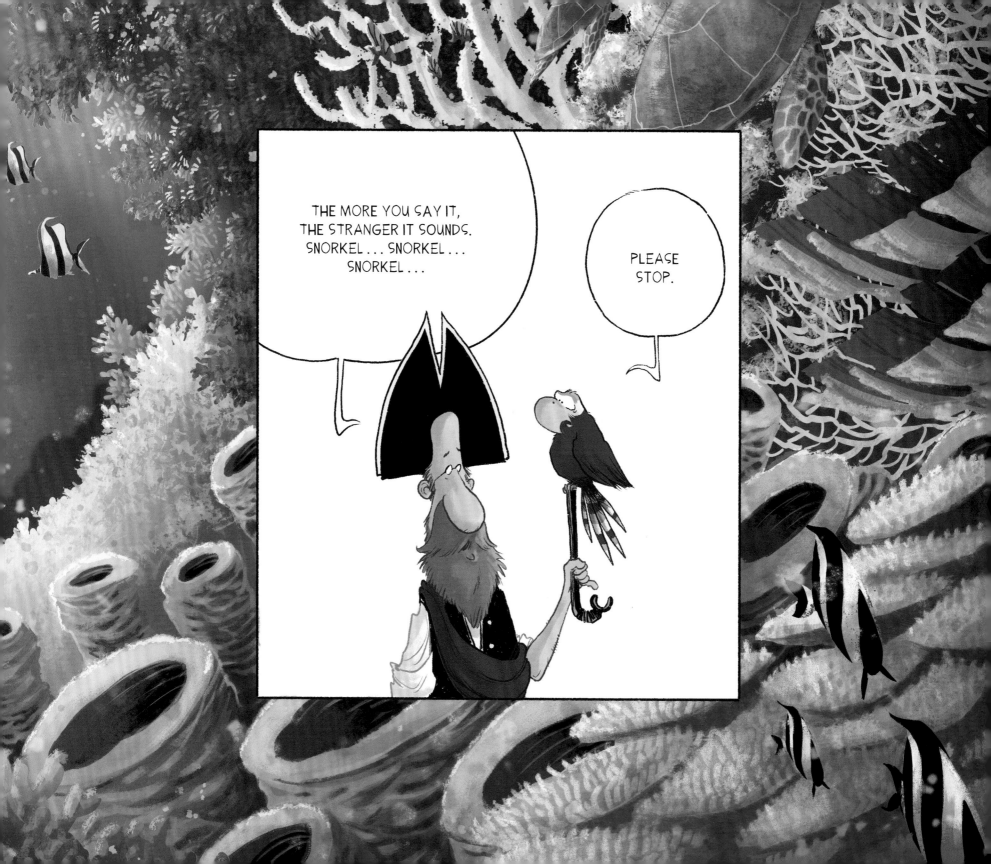

On a recent trip to the Challenger Deep,
researchers hoped to make new discoveries
about the deepest place on the planet.
You'll never guess what they found instead. . . .

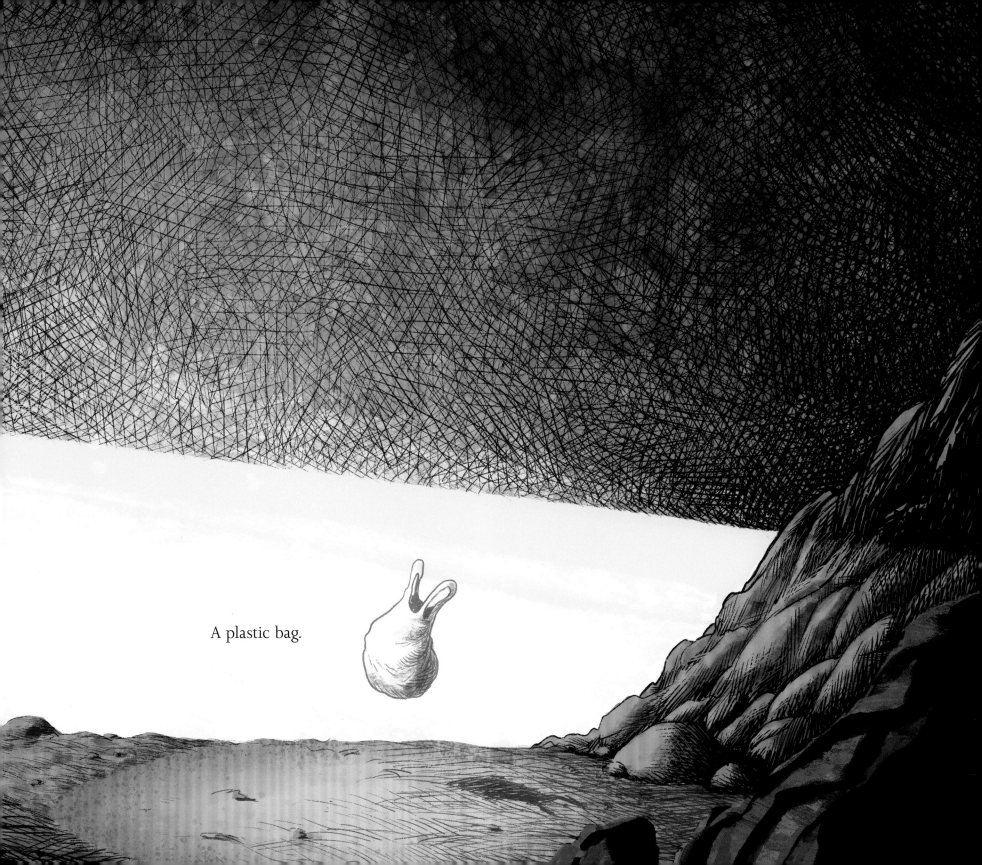

A plastic bag.

The ocean is in danger.

Pollution, climate change, and overfishing are putting these amazing ecosystems at risk.

Imagine what we might find in the 90 percent of the ocean we haven't explored yet.

YOU ARE MORE LIKELY TO BE BITTEN BY A HIPPOPOTAMUS THAN A SHARK.

NOT COOL, GARY.

Ocean

HIT ME.

I THINK YOU'VE HAD ENOUGH.

FISH REST BUT DON'T SLEEP.

THE AVERAGE TEMPERATURE OF DEEP OCEAN WATER, MORE THAN 650 FEET DEEP, GLOBALLY IS 39 DEGREES FAHRENHEIT.